INCA EMPI

A History from Beginning to End

Copyright © 2020 by Hourly History.

All rights reserved.

Table of Contents

Introduction
The Andean Civilizations
Origin of the Incas
The Kingdom of Cuzco
The Rise of the Empire
Life in the Inca Empire
The Spanish Conquest
The Fall of the Inca Empire
Conclusion

Introduction

In the early fifteenth century, the Incas were a small tribe who lived in a series of villages in a single valley in the southern highlands of present-day Peru. Within less than one hundred years, they became the dominant power in South America, ruling lands which included over ten million subjects. They also built mighty cities as well as roads and irrigation systems so advanced that they are still in use today.

In the 1500s, the Inca Empire was utterly destroyed by a small number of Spanish invaders and the diseases they brought with them. Few empires in the history of the world have risen so high, so quickly and then been destroyed in such a short space of time.

The Incas were effective warriors and priests and innovative artists, scientists, and architects. Above all, however, they were superlative administrators; as few as forty thousand Incas ruled over an empire of many millions. Until the coming of the Spanish invaders, it seemed that nothing could block the power and growth of the Inca Empire. Then, just as abruptly as it had emerged, the empire was gone, replaced by colonial overlords who brought with them new technologies and new ways of life.

In historical terms, the Inca Empire lasted little more than the blink of an eye. Yet it managed to develop art and infrastructure that continue to be relevant today. This is the story of the rapid rise and sudden collapse of the mighty Inca Empire.

Chapter One

The Andean Civilizations

"We are not myths of the past, ruins in the jungle, or zoos. We are people and we want to be respected, not to be victims of intolerance and racism."

—Rigoberta Menchu Tum

The last ice age began to loosen its grip on the planet around 10,000-12,000 years ago. Vast tracts of land which had been covered by ice were slowly revealed and people began to enter areas where there had never been humans before. Some of these people, loose affiliations of hunter-gatherers, crossed from present-day Siberia to present-day Alaska via the Bering Land Bridge. As the ice melted, sea levels rose and the land bridge was gradually submerged under the Bering Strait. The people who had crossed were unable to return to Siberia and they began to move south and east into North America as melting glaciers revealed more and more land.

Some of these people settled in present-day Canada and down the west coast of present-day United States. These Native Americans developed their own societies, cultures, and ways of life, and some people went even further south into South America. They spread down the west coast of the continent, in the area between the Andes Mountains and the Pacific Ocean in parts of present-day Chile, Peru,

Bolivia, and Ecuador. There they formed what have become known as the Andean civilizations. These people were mainly farmers and fishermen, living in villages near the coast or close to the rivers which flow from the Andes to the Pacific. The coastal area was largely dry desert, so life must have been very difficult for these early settlers.

Some of the incomers settled instead in the high Andes. There were no deserts there, but climatic conditions were still extremely inhospitable. In the area around Lake Titicaca, the largest lake in South America, there were many small communities. This area is 12,500 feet (3,800 meters) above sea level. There is frost here on average three hundred nights every year and temperatures can vary by up 70 °F within twenty-four hours. This is not an easy place in which to live, and yet many of the early people of South America settled in this or similar areas.

In addition to farming, these people also raised domesticated herds of llama and alpaca. While the llama is a hardy animal that can thrive almost anywhere, the alpaca does best at over 13,000 feet above sea level. These animals were raised mainly for their wool which was used to produce textiles.

By around 8000 BCE, there were well-established human settlements in this area, particularly in the highlands of the Andes. By 3500 BCE, human settlement in coastal areas was widespread with farmers growing maize and beans and undertaking extensive fishing in the sea and in rivers and lakes. Progress was relatively slow for the next thousand years, and by 2500 BCE, there were no more than one hundred villages on the coast and even the largest had a population of fewer than one thousand people.

By 1500 BCE, there were much more sophisticated human settlements and this period saw the first cultures to spread across the area. From around 3000 BCE to 1800 BCE, the Caral civilization (also known as the Norte Chico) spread across thirty towns and cities in present-day coastal Peru. Little is known about this period, though this civilization produced the first monumental architecture in the area, with large sunken plazas and earthwork mounds the purpose of which is still unknown. The Chavin culture emerged around 1500 BCE and is named after the Chavin de Huantar temple complex discovered in the Andes Mountains of Peru. Investigation of this site has revealed that it was the center of a thriving community living in permanent houses which included some buildings made from worked blocks of stone. The community was involved in producing ceramics and textiles.

The Nazca people thrived in the southern coastal area of present-day Peru from around 100 to 800 CE. This society produced complex and beautiful ceramics and textiles and built a system of underground aqueducts so sophisticated that many are still in use today. This society is probably best remembered today for its production of complex geoglyphs, lines, symbols, and designs created in the Nazca Desert by digging trenches to uncover lighter substrata. These designs are of unknown purpose and are generally called the "Nazca Lines."

Contemporary with the Nazca civilization, in the north of present-day Peru, was the Moche civilization. We aren't certain if this was a single entity governed by an administrative center or simply a group of autonomous states which shared common beliefs, but this civilization left a number of large stone buildings and was a producer of high-quality ceramics and textiles. Evidence suggests that there at least some trade between the Moche and the Nazca civilizations.

In the south-central Andes there was another culture, the Wari, centered around the city of Wari in present-day Peru. The Wari built a number of small cities and established several administrative centers in the region, and they controlled and built a road network to connect these.

By around 750 CE, the Moche and Nazca civilizations were in decline, and by around 800 CE, all seem to have vanished completely. No-one is completely certain what caused the simultaneous collapse of these civilizations, though it has been noted that there appear to have been extreme climatic changes for a period of around 50 years up to 600 CE including flooding and then several consecutive years of drought. It has also been noted that archeological investigations reveal that Moche cities after 600 CE have elaborate fortifications, something that had not previously displayed. This suggests either an invasion of some sort or perhaps a scarcity of resources which led to fighting between factions. The Wari culture seems to have lasted a little longer, but by 1000 CE, it too had virtually disappeared.

In present-day Bolivia, near Lake Titicaca, the remains of a city larger than any of those built by the Moche or the Nazca have been discovered. This city, Tiwanaku (also known as Tiahuanaco) covered more than four square kilometers and is thought to have been the home to up to twenty thousand people at around the time that the Moche and Nazca were disappearing. The city itself featured large buildings and plazas, often built from enormous blocks of stone—the largest block weighed over 65 metric tons. Excavation has also revealed fine ceramics and it is thought that a city existed on this site from around 100 BCE for more than one thousand years.

However, just like the history of most of the pre-Inca Andean civilizations, we know almost nothing about the people who built and lived in Tiwanaku. It is believed that they may have controlled large areas of present-day Peru, but none of the ancient Andean civilizations developed systems of writing, so all we know about their societies, beliefs, and cultures are what we can deduce from archeological excavation. What we do know is that the civilizations which developed in this area are classed by historians as "pristine," that is to say that they developed in isolation, without influence from other civilizations. We also know that they did not seem to have money or any equivalent—any trade which took place must have involved barter rather than cash.

We also know that these people were mainly farmers and fishermen and that agriculture must have been very difficult due to the landscape and climate in the areas where they lived. The arid coastal plains required complex irrigation systems to make them viable locations for growing crops and the high Andes required the building of terraces and the exploitation of micro-climates to produce crops. Many of the Andean cultures exploited what historians have called the "vertical archipelago" approach, where a single culture had settlements at a number of levels, from the sea to the high mountains, in order to extract as much use as possible from a difficult landscape.

Before the Incas became a major force in the region, another Andean culture grew out of the disintegration of the Moche culture. The Kingdom of Chimor was centered around the city of Chan Chan in present-day Peru. This appears to have been the first true empire in the region. The cultures which had gone before seem to have been largely voluntary groupings of people who shared common beliefs and languages. Although Chimor began this way with a grouping of descendants of the Moche people in around 900 CE, it grew by conquest until it dominated more than one thousand kilometers of the coastline of South America.

Chimor was ruled by an elite group who organized life in the cities and lands controlled by their armies. Engineering works were undertaken to build fortifications, canals, and irrigation systems, and raw materials were imported into Chan Chan where artisans produced fine textiles, ceramics, and metalwork (it has been estimated that up to 12,000 artisans may have lived and worked in the city). The city itself had more than 25,000 inhabitants, most of whom lived in *barrios* on the outer edges while the ruling elite lived in ten royal compounds, *ciudadelas*, each protected by tall adobe walls.

The Kingdom of Chimor continued to be the dominant power in the region for more than 600 years, until an obscure tribe in a small mountain valley grew powerful enough to challenge their control.

Chapter Two

Origin of the Incas

"Don't lie, don't cheat, don't be lazy."

—Quechua greeting

Like the other people of the Andes, the tribe which would become the Incas had no written language, so what we know of their history comes mainly from oral tradition or from written histories produced after the arrival of Europeans in South America. These people believed that they were directly descended from the creator god Viracocha who came from the Pacific Ocean to Lake Titicaca where he created the sun. The sun god, Inti, then created people, the "Children of the Sun," at Tiwanaku and these people moved almost five hundred miles to the north to the Valley of Cuzco, where they defeated the indigenous people in battle and established their capital, the city of Cuzco.

Cuzco (the name is thought to derive from the local word *qosqo*, meaning "dried-up lakebed") lies in a natural basin formed by glaciers and near a dried-up lakebed which was also the confluence of three rivers, the Huatanay, the Tullumayo and the Chunchul. This location was also an important junction joining several significant trade routes. Excavations have shown that this area was first occupied by humans about 4500 BCE, but what would become the city of Cuzco was not established until much later, perhaps around 1000 CE. The valley in which the city is situated is over 10,000 feet above sea level but provides fertile agricultural land, and the surrounding mountain peaks provide grazing for domesticated animals.

By around 1300 CE, Cuzco had become an important city-state. The people who lived there had astonishing architectural skills, especially in working giant blocks of stone. These were worked so accurately that they were fitted together without mortar to create gigantic walls. At the heart of the city was the Golden Enclosure (Coricancha), the most important religious site and regarded by the inhabitants of the city as the center of the world. Inside was a complex of temples dedicated to various gods including Viracocha, Inti, and the moon goddess, Mama Kilya.

With outer walls built of huge stone blocks, the interior of these temples must have been an astonishing sight—many doors and walls were completely covered in beaten gold and some were also studded with emeralds. The interior walls of the Temple of Inti, for example, were covered with more than seven hundred two-kilogram sheets of gold while the interior of the Temple of Mama Kilya was similarly covered with sheets of beaten silver.

Most stunning of all was the Coricancha garden which featured a life-size field of corn, gardeners, and animals including llamas, jaguars, guinea pigs, monkeys, birds, and even butterflies and insects, all made from gold or silver and all studded with precious stones. The Coricancha also featured an underground aqueduct through which water made sacred in the temple complex was routed to fountains and wells throughout the city which featured large squares, canals, and open parkland.

The Kingdom of Cuzco, which in its earliest times comprised little more than the city itself and the valley in which it was located, was ruled over from around 1200 CE by a ruler known variously as the Apu ("divine one"), the Sapa ("mighty one") and Sapa Inca ("only Inca"). This ruler was revered as a god-like being who was the offspring of the sun god Inti. The position was hereditary, being passed from father to son. This ruler was not just the head of state but also the leader of the city-state's religion. The Sapa Inca had several wives and the principal wife was known as the Coya and this woman had an important ceremonial role in the royal household.

All land under the control of the city of Cuzco belonged to the Sapa Inca and could be distributed by him to any of three distinct groups: followers and retainers of the Sapa Inca, including court functionaries and military leaders, the priesthood, for the construction of temples and other religious sites, and to the common people for use as farming or grazing land. The ultimate ownership of the land remained with the Sapa Inca and the granting of its use for a particular purpose could be revoked if he was displeased.

The first recorded Sapa Inca was Manco Cápac who was said to have first led his people to the Valley of Cuzco, defeated the indigenous people there, and established the city of Cuzco. It is not clear if he was a real or mythological figure—Manco Cápac was defined in Inca tradition as the son of the god Viracocha. Tradition relates how this leader arrived in the Valley of Cuzco with a relatively small band of followers, defeated the three local tribes (the Sahuares, the Huallas, and the Alcahuisas) with the help of warriors created from local stones, and then decided to establish a permanent settlement in a swampy area between two rivers, the area which would become the central square of Cuzco.

Manco Cápac was succeeded by his son, Sinchi Roca, who began a tradition that was continued by all succeeding Sapa Incas; he built a new royal palace in the city rather than using the palace used by his predecessor. Under his rule, the Kingdom of Cuzco became established, the city began to grow, and a program of improvements were started which included the terracing of agricultural land and the importation of large quantities of good soil from land at lower altitude to improve farming. The names of the first Sapa Incas became incorporated into the language used by the people of Cuzco, Quechua: *Sinchi* came to be used as a title for a mayor or local leader, and *Cápac* came to mean a warlord or military leader.

Sinchi Roca was followed as Sapa Inca by his son, Lloque Yupanqui ("the left-handed deity") who came to the throne around 1260 CE. Like his father and grandfather before him, this ruler concentrated on improvements to the city rather than trying to expand its area of influence.

In 1290, the fourth Sapa Inca, Mayta Cápac, succeeded his father. Inca legend suggests that this was the first Inca leader to conquer other lands, but investigation by historians and archeological excavations show that this was not so. Under his rule, two adjacent regions, Arequipa and Moquegua, did come under some measure of control from Cuzco, though it appears that this was part of a series of trade treaties rather than an act of conquest.

In 1320, Mayta Cápac was succeeded by his son, Cápac Yupanqui ("splendid accountant Inca"). As his name suggests, this leader spent most of his time on improvements in the city of Cuzco, building aqueducts, public buildings, roads, canals, and bridges. He did manage to subjugate two of the other tribes who shared the Cuzco Valley with the people of the city of Cuzco. The Cuyumarca and Ancasmarca had been a constant source of irritation, raiding domestic animals and disrupting trade and farming outside the city. During the reign of Cápac Yupanqui, both were brought under the domination of Cuzco, and the Cuzco Valley fell entirely under the control of the city of Cuzco.

By the time of the death of Cápac Yupanqui, the society in the city of Cuzco had become clearly divided into two distinct social groupings (often called *moities*): the *hanan*, who were chiefly associated with military matters, and the *hurin* (or *urin*), who were mainly associated with the priesthood. The first five Sapa Incas were supported by the hurin. When Cápac Yupanqui died in 1350, he was expected to be succeeded by his eldest son, Quispe Yupanqui. However, before he could take the throne, there was a revolt by the hanan moiety and Quispe Yupanqui was killed. His place was taken by his half-brother, Inca Roca (who was said in some accounts to have provided the poison which killed Quispe Yupanqui), who was supported by the hanan moiety. All the Sapa Incas who followed were supported by the hanan rather than the hurin. This is significant because all the Sapa Incas who followed were notably more interested in military matters and conquest than their predecessors.

Chapter Three

The Kingdom of Cuzco

"The Inca were the Romans of the New World."

—The Great Inca Rebellion

Inca Roca quickly proved to be an effective leader. He ordered the channeling of the Huatanay River and the building of canals to ensure that the four districts of the city were provided with a plentiful supply of water. He also created schools where the young men of Cuzco could be trained in military matters as well as the basics of accounting and knowledge of the history of their city and its people.

He also began for the first time to challenge tribes outside the Cuzco Valley, mounting successful raids against the neighboring city-states to the south of Cuzco including Quiquijan and Caitomarca and to the city of Paucartambo to the east. The purpose of these raids was to seize food, textiles, and cattle and bring them back to Cuzco. There was no attempt to mount any form of permanent occupation of the conquered cities of territories, and when the booty was seized, the cities were left to continue as before.

Inca Roca married Mama Micay, daughter of the ruler of the city-state of Huallacán. This marriage caused dissent because it was claimed that Mama Micay had already been promised to the ruler of the Ayarmaca tribe. A series of conflicts between Cuzco and Ayarmaca followed, and an uneasy peace was achieved only when the son of Inca Roca and Mama Micay, Tito Cusí Huallpa, was given as a hostage to the Ayarmaca. Inca legend has it that the Ayarmaca initially intended to kill the little boy but changed their minds when they saw that he wept tears of blood. Eventually, the boy was released, and a lasting peace between the people of Cuzco and the Ayarmaca was agreed when a daughter of Inca Roca married the king of the Ayarmaca and Inca Roca took a princess from the Ayarmaca as one of his wives.

Inca Roca ruled for 30 years, and during that time, the city of Cuzco was improved and the power and military might of the people who were coming to be called the Incas grew. When he died in 1380, there was great mourning in the city of Cuzco and in the lands over which it had gained control.

Inca Roca was succeeded by his 19-year-old son Tito Cusí Huallpa, who took the title Yawar Waqaq Inka ("the Inca who cries blood") when he ascended to power, in memory of the time he had spent as a hostage to the Ayarmaca. From the very beginning, the reign of Yawar Waqaq was difficult. He faced an uprising by the Pinagua tribe who had previously seemed content to live under Inca rule. This was put down by his brother, Vicaquirao, a competent military leader who was one of the first Incas to understand that it was best to leave an occupying force behind in conquered territory, ensuring compliance and a continuing flow of tribute.

Continuing friction with the Ayarmaca tribe was at least partly solved by a marriage to a woman from the royal house of the tribe, Mama Chiquia. The Sapa Inca had many children with this wife including his favorite son, Paguac Huallpa, who he also nominated as his heir. However, this angered the people of the city-state of Paullo, main home of the Huallacán tribe, who had hoped that Yawar Waqaq would choose as his successor Marcayuto, whose mother had come from Paullo. They invited Paguac Huallpa to visit Paullo, but while he was there he was murdered. Angered by the killing of his son, Yawar Waqaq sent an army to Paullo. The city was quickly conquered and sacked, and many important members of the Huallacán tribe were killed in retaliation.

Yawar Waqaq then had to contend with a larger and much stronger insurrection by the Cunti tribe, whose lands had been occupied by armies led by Vicaquirao. The Cuntis mounted a successful attack on the city of Cuzco and succeeded in capturing and killing the Sapa Inca. However, the Cuntis did not remain in occupation—they soon left Cuzco to return to their own lands. Inca legend tells of a huge storm which ravaged the city soon after its conquest, persuading the Cuntis that the gods were displeased and that they should leave.

Another tribe previously under control of the Incas, the Chankas, also seized the opportunity to stage a successful revolt against Inca rule, expelling the Inca occupying forces and regaining control of their lands. By the time of the death of Yawar Waqaq, the Kingdom of Cuzco had lost control over almost everything except lands within the Cuzco Valley.

After the Cuntis had left the city, the surviving hanan gathered to choose a successor. They chose a young man, Hatun Tupac, who was a son or nephew of Yawar Waqaq. He took the title Viracocha Inca because, he said, he had dreamed of the god Quechua and of conquering "all of the world" for the Inca. Initially, he was able to extend the area controlled by Cuzco easily, conquering the city states of Yucay and Calca and fighting a successful war against the Ayarmaca. However, Viracocha Inca was not a popular ruler, and his situation was made worse when he appointed his son Urco as his heir and the leader of important religious and military groups. Urco was said to be addicted to alcohol and was frequently to be seen drunk, vomiting, and urinating in the streets of the city. He also frequented brothels in the city and was said to have raped more than one high-born woman. Despite these faults, Viracocha Inca could not be persuaded to nominate a different heir.

Then, the lands of Cuzco were invaded again by the Chanka people, an ethnic group from lands centered around the city-state of Andahuaylas. The Chankas had a fearsome reputation as warriors, being fierce in battle and merciless to those they captured. It was not uncommon for prisoners to be slowly skinned alive and their skulls to be made into drinking cups. The Chankas swept through the Inca lands until they arrived at the walls of the city of Cuzco. Viracocha Inca and his son Urco fled from the city, taking their wives and retinues with them. They believed that resistance was useless and that it was inevitable that the city would fall.

However, Viracocha Inca had another son, Cusi Yupanqui, who was determined to stay in the city and to fight the Chankas. He gathered the remaining Incas forces and not only stopped the Chankas from taking the city, but he also expelled them from all Inca lands. He then pursued the Chankas back into their native lands and attacked and sacked their principal city, Andahuaylas. He brought back to Cuzco an immense booty, including many Chanka prisoners who were massacred as part of the victory celebrations.

Jealous of the prestige this brought his brother, Urco planned to have Cusí Yupanqui murdered, but the plot failed and instead Urco was killed. Prostrated by grief and reviled because of his decision to abandon the city, Viracocha Inca was persuaded to abdicate and Cusí Yupanqui became the new Sapa Inca in 1438, taking the title Pachacuti Inca ("the Inca who shakes the earth"). From this point on, Cuzco would change from a small kingdom to a mighty empire in a remarkably short space of time.

Chapter Four

The Rise of the Empire

"I was born as a lily in the garden, and like the lily I grew, as my age advanced. I became old and had to die, and so I withered and died."

—Song attributed to Pachacuti

Almost as soon as he became Sapa Inca, Pachacuti set about transforming the Kingdom of Cuzco. He was a very able military leader, having served under his uncle, Vicaquirao, during his successful campaigns. He set out on a campaign of conquest, and for the first four years of his reign, he won victory after victory, conquering the Ayarmacas, the Amaybamba, the Vitcos, and the Vilcabamba. Other tribes and ethnic groups in the area became nervous of Inca military success and several, including the Cotapampa, the Cotanera, the Omasayo, and the Aimarae, voluntarily concluded treaties that made them part of the growing Inca Empire.

In many of the areas he conquered, Pachacuti established regional centers which exerted control over these new lands once the main armies had left. These included Vilcashuamán in the region of Huamanga, and on the Pacific coast, he founded Incahuasi after a short campaign in which the tribes of Chincha, Huarco, and Lunahuaná were defeated.

The seemingly inexorable advance of the Incas continued in a later campaign in the northern highlands of present-day Peru, this time in alliance with the Chankas, which led to the defeat of the Collas. By the time that Pachacuti had finished his program of conquest, he ruled not a kingdom but an empire, the *Tawantinsuyu* ("the four regions"), which covered a large part of western South America.

Pachacuti also made sweeping changes to the city of Cuzco. Many public buildings were rebuilt on a larger scale, the marshes which had surrounded the city were drained, prisons were built to hold those who opposed Pachacuti's autocratic rule, and the Coricancha was made even more opulent.

Pachacuti also undertook other construction projects outside the Valley of Cuzco. The astonishing fortress at Machu Picchu in the Eastern Cordillera of southern Peru was built as an estate for Pachacuti in around 1450. Massive fortresses and temples were built in several locations around the empire including Pisac and Ollantaytambo at either end of the Urubamba Valley. These were used as garrisons for Inca troops to ensure that conquered people did not rebel.

The city of Cuzco itself was divided into four quarters, reflecting the four regions (*suyus*) of the empire. Each quarter of the city was dedicated to the region which it faced, and all administrative and economic functions associated with a particular region were concentrated in that part of the city. Any settlers or envoys from a particular region were housed in the corresponding part of the city. Cuzco became the center of the empire and, as far as the Incas were concerned, the center of the world.

Much of the building work undertaken by the Incas in Cuzco and elsewhere involved the quarrying and transport of huge blocks of stone which were then worked so precisely that they could be fitted together without the use of mortar. Even now, historians have no idea how this was achieved, especially since some of the blocks weighed over 50 tons. How these were quarried, transported, worked, and then lifted into place is one of the major mysteries surrounding the Incas. The fortress of fortress of Sacsayhuaman, for example, which was built on the orders of Pachacuti to guard the northern approaches to Cuzco, has external walls entirely constructed of massive stone blocks.

Pachacuti also introduced new laws, especially laws which required all members of Inca society to perform compulsory service to the state (*mita*) which might involve military service or working as labor on state construction projects or even farming. He also began a policy of forced migration, making thousands of Incas of the lowest classes relocate to the most remote areas of the new empire. These *mitimaes* were used to enforce Inca rule of conquered lands but also to spread Inca ideas, religions, and cultures to new areas. All speakers of the Inca language, Quechua, were made citizens of the Inca Empire, something that gave even the lowest class Inca a boost in status over any of the conquered people.

One of the things that the mitimaes were expected to do was to ensure the supply of tribute from conquered areas back to the city of Cuzco. Tributes might be in the form of gold or food or might be provided as labor for work on state construction projects. All conquered areas were expected to pay for the privilege of being part of the Inca Empire. This was unpopular, but the Incas did provide benefits in return. They built a complex system of roads across the empire, making travel faster and safer, and Pachacuti also had built a system of warehouses—the *qollqa*. These heavily guarded buildings were used to store surplus food and could distribute this when there were shortages so that starvation became less common in the Inca Empire. The qollqa were carefully and cleverly designed and built in areas where they would be permanently cool, and it was said to possible to store even perishable food in their storehouses for up to four years.

Towards the end of his reign, Pachacuti retired to his royal palace in Cuzco; rule of the empire, and responsibility for new conquests, passed to his son, Topa Inca Yupanqui, who was appointed leader of the Inca army in 1463. For around eight years, Pachacuti and his son appear to have equitably co-ruled the empire until Pachacuti's death in 1471. According to his orders, the empire entered a one-year period of mourning. A mock battle was held at Cuzco in commemoration, and festivals and sacrifices took place across the empire—children were sacrificed in every place that Pachacuti had visited during his lifetime.

When Topa Inca Yupanqui became leader of the Incas, he continued the conquests started by his father, extending the area controlled by the Incas to much of South America. He led expeditions to conquer new lands from the Chimor, a people who lived in the coastal area of present-day northern Peru, and to the east where he conquered the province of Antis. Like his father, the new Sapa Inca built garrisons and fortresses in conquered lands to ensure that they remained under Inca control and continued to provide tribute to the empire.

Topa Inca Yupanqui also created two new administrative centers which became responsible for control and taxation of conquered lands, one in the city of Xauxa and the other in the city of Tiahuanacu. Both were ruled by governor generals (*Suyuyoc Apu*), and both became important regional centers in the Inca Empire.

It is also said that Topa Inca Yupanqui undertook a long voyage of discovery in the Pacific Ocean. Inca legend tells of how he had a fleet of seagoing vessels called *balsas* made from woven totora reeds and on these he embarked an army of 20,000 troops. He then set sail on a voyage which lasted for so long (some accounts say nine months, some over one year) that many of his subjects believed him to be dead.

During this voyage, Topa Inca Yupanqui was said to have discovered two groups of islands, which he named *Nina Chumpi* ("fire belt") and *Hawa Chumpi* ("outer belt"). Some people have claimed that Topa Inca Yupanqui reached the Galapagos Islands, though many historians are skeptical that the voyage ever really took place at all. It is notable, however, that the people who live on Easter Island, far out in the Pacific, have an oral tradition that once in the distant past their island was visited by strange people from another land, the *hanau eepe*, and there has been speculation that this actually refers to a visit by the Sapa Inca and his followers.

Topa Inca Yupanqui also extended the system of roads started by his father and ordered extensive construction work in the city of Quito, the capital of present-day Ecuador, located in the fertile Guayllabamba River basin. He brought in architects and builders from Cuzco to ensure that Quito, for which he seemed to have a particular fondness, had monumental temples and palaces to rival those of the Inca capital.

Topa Inca Yupanqui died in 1493, leaving two legitimate sons and more than ninety illegitimate children. He nominated as his heir one of these illegitimate children, Capac Huari. However, Capac Huari and his mother, the royal concubine Chuqui Ocllo, both died soon after the death of Topa Inca Yupanqui. The precise circumstances of their deaths are not known, but it is assumed that they were murdered in order that one of the Sapa Inca's legitimate children, Titu Cusi Huallpa, would become Inca emperor, taking the title Huayna Capac.

The new emperor quickly began expanding the Inca Empire even further. The Confederation of Quito (in present-day Ecuador) was brought into the Inca Empire by the marriage of Huayna Capac to the Quito Queen Paccha Duchicela Shyris XVI. Other additions were made by conquest in areas to the south of Cuzco, in present-day Chile and Argentina and to the north in present-day Columbia. Under the rule of Huayna Capac, the Inca Empire reached its greatest extent, stretching more than 1,000 miles from north to south and incorporating more than 200 distinct ethnic groups comprising around 14 million people ruled by around 100,000 Incas.

The road system was extended further during this period, the system of storage warehouses was improved, and several new construction projects were undertaken which included the building of more than 2,000 silos for grain storage at the city of Cochabamba in present-day Bolivia and the construction of an astronomical observatory in the city of Ingapirca in present-day Ecuador.

When Huayna Capac died of a fever in 1524, the Inca Empire was vast, secure, sophisticated, and seemed destined to last for a very long time. No-one could have guessed that he would be the last Sapa Inca to end his rule with the empire intact. The destruction of the empire would be even more rapid than its rise.

Chapter Five

Life in the Inca Empire

"The Incas' genius— like that of the Romans—lay in their masterful organizational abilities. Amazingly, an ethnic group that probably never exceeded 100,000 individuals was able to regulate the activities of roughly ten million people."

—Kim MacQuarrie, The Last Days of the Incas

The government of the Inca Empire was autocratic and controlling in the extreme. Even the clothing which its citizens wore was defined and supplied by the state. Each Inca was provided with two sets of clothes—a tunic for everyday use, made from *Awaska* cloth woven from llama wool and another made from finer cloth, *qunpi,* often woven from alpaca wool, for formal or ceremonial occasions. These were worn until they were reduced to rags as no Inca was permitted to change or replace their clothing without permission. These tunics incorporated a geometric design which indicated the status of the wearer—for example, members of the army wore tunics decorated with a black and white checkered pattern.

People of special importance also wore a turban-like hat which incorporated designs and colors which denoted the family to which they belonged. These *llawt'u* also denoted the social standing of the wearer—the finer the cloth and more intricate the design, the wealthier the individual. In order to stress his importance, one Sapa Inca had a llawt'u made entirely from hair taken from vampire bats.

The designs which decorated clothes were also used on ceramics, wood carvings, and metalwork. Like every other aspect of Inca life, these designs were standardized and set by the state. Inca designs generally incorporated simple geometrical shapes, sometimes enlivened by simplified representations of animals. These formed an instantly recognizable imperial design which was replicated throughout the empire.

The government itself was headed by the Sapa Inca who was responsible for making all important decisions. He was assisted by a council comprising representatives from ten important Inca families. These *panaqa* were also involved in ratifying the Sapa Inca's choice of his successor. Next in importance to the *panaqa* were the representatives of ten more groups taken from slightly less influential families (or from families with a less direct blood connection to the Sapa Inca). Then there were representatives of noble families who were not Incas, but whose assimilation into the Inca Empire made them important. There was no formal system of government or advising, and there was often great rivalry between these various group of nobles for the attention of the Sapa Inca.

Each of the four quarters of the empire was administered by a regional governor who had under his control up to 80 local administrators, generally ethnic Incas. Below these Incas were *kurakas*, nobles from the local area who were often not themselves ethnic Incas. One of the functions of local administrators was the taking of a regular census on which the level of tribute was based. This was overseen and checked by an inspector appointed by the regional governor, the *tokoyrikoq* ("he who sees all"). These records were not kept in writing (the Incas had no written language) but in the form of *quipu*, a complex arrangement of knots and strings which was easily transportable and capable of recording numbers up to 10,000.

Because the Incas had no currency, tribute was paid in kind, often in the form of food but sometimes also in metals or in the form of labor which could be used on state projects. The loyalty of local nobles was often assured by taking their heirs or close family members as hostages in Cuzco.

One notable feature of the rigid centralized control exerted by the Inca rulers was a lack of marketplaces and an almost complete absence of trade or any form of merchant class within Inca society. The Sapa Inca provided all his subjects with food, and in return, all citizens were expected to give some of their time to projects on behalf of the state. Just like the clothing they wore, the food that the majority of Incas and subject people consumed was provided by and chosen by the government.

One of the most significant Inca construction projects was the system of roads which they built to connect the disparate parts of the empire. The Inca royal roads (*qhapaqñan*) extended for over 25,000 miles and included not just well-designed and built roads but also bridges, stairways, and causeways. The road system comprised two main routes, both running north-south, one near the coast and the other running through the Andes. Lesser routes branched off these to link all the main administrative centers and storage areas within the empire. The system included lodging houses (*tambos*) approximately every 15 miles and smaller rest stops (*chaskiwasi*) where travelers had access to clean drinking water.

Major roads incorporated stone markers giving distances to important destinations in *topo* (one topo equals approximately five miles). The construction of some of these roads represented an astonishing engineering feat, with roads clinging to the side of sheer cliffs, spanning deep ravines, and crossing high mountain passes. Roads were not intended for the use or ordinary citizens of the empire—this was only allowed with special permission from a local governor, and tolls were charged at bridges and other points.

Although the Incas had no wheeled vehicles, perishable items including food could be transported surprising distances by using relays of trained runners (*chaski*) to carry them on these roads. It was said to be possible to transport baskets of fresh fish, for example, 150 miles in a single day.

It was the responsibility of local governors to ensure that roads were kept in good repair and free of obstructions at all times. The labor required to do this formed part of the tribute each area was expected to contribute to the central administration. Inca roads were so well laid out and built that some are still in use today, and even some modern roads are built over the routes first established by Inca roads.

Inca religion permeated every aspect of daily life and involved a bewildering array of gods and animistic spirits.

The principal gods included the creator Viracocha, the sun god Inti, and the moon goddess Mama Kilya. There were also a host of other gods in a complex hierarchy, some of whom resided in heaven while some lived on earth. Each crop, for example, was considered to have its own protective spirit (*conopas*), and anything up to one-third of each harvest was set aside as an offering to these spirits. Domestic animals also had their own protective spirits (*illas*), and small effigies of animals would be buried under yards and animal pens to appease these spirits.

The deities who inhabited mountains were considered especially important because these were believed to control such things as rainfall and flooding and were therefore very important to agriculture. Ritual human sacrifices were carried out to appease these deities, and these often involved the victims being buried alive on mountainsides.

Communication with the gods was done through shamans who both officiated at religious ceremonies and acted as healers, often using herbs in conjunction with appeasement of the gods. Illnesses were not considered to be purely physical, but to be a manifestation of a spiritual problem which could only be fully cured with the assistance of the gods and spirits and not just by treating the body. It appears that the Inca shamans even developed some advanced surgical techniques. For examples, skulls have been recovered from this period which show signs of being drilled or even having sections removed entirely. This technique, called trepanation, seems to have been used to treat combat injuries and the subsequent growth of bones suggest that the shaman surgeons were sufficiently skilled that their patients survived this delicate and dangerous surgery for many years.

Most roles in government and the military were undertaken by men in Inca society, though women were permitted to be local governors. Lower-class men were allowed just one wife but those of the higher classes, including the Sapa Inca, were permitted to have many wives. One unusual feature of Inca society was the existence of trial marriages. A man and woman could decide to live together as man and wife for an agreed period, usually more than one year. At the end of this period, each was free to decide not to proceed to marriage. If both agreed, the marriage would be declared final. Once a man and woman were married, a divorce could only be arranged if the woman failed to bear any children.

The food which Incas ate was largely vegetarian (except in coastal areas where fish was eaten) due to a scarcity of meat. A kind of porridge made from quinoa was a staple food for ordinary people. Potatoes were also widely eaten, especially in the form of *chuno*, made by freeze-drying potatoes at high altitude, which allows them to be stored for up to four years. Most ordinary people ate just two meals each day, one in the early morning and one late at night, often accompanied by *chicha*, an alcoholic beer-like beverage.

Overall, Inca society was much more rigidly controlled than almost any other previous or subsequent empire. Almost every aspect of life for ordinary Incas and the subject people they ruled was defined and administered by the state. This provided the empire with stability. Central control of agriculture and the roads and warehouse system, for example, ensured that food could be transported throughout the empire to prevent shortages and starvation. But it also meant that there was no chance of change or any form of social mobility—the lack of trade, markets, or even money meant that it was virtually impossible for someone born to a low-class family to advance up the social ladder.

Chapter Six

The Spanish Conquest

"I have come to take away their gold."

—Francisco Pizarro

If the rise of the Inca Empire was startling in the speed with which it was achieved, its complete destruction was even more astoundingly rapid. When Huayna Capac died in 1524, there seems to have been confusion (or at least dispute) about who should succeed him. Huayna Capac had named his infant son, Ninan Cuyochi, as his heir. However, the boy died of the same fever which killed his father. This left two of Huayna Capac's sons, Huáscar and Atahualpa, as logical successors.

Huáscar was supported by a faction based in Cuzco while Atahualpa was favored by another faction based in the north of the empire. No agreement was reached, and the empire descended into a bloody civil war as two Inca armies, each of around 60,000 men, faced each other in a series of battles. After years of bitter fighting, the forces supporting Atahualpa were triumphant and in 1532, Cuzco was captured and occupied and Huáscar was imprisoned.

At that moment, a new force appeared in the lands of the Incas. In the late 1400s, Christopher Columbus had discovered the Americas on behalf of the Spanish Crown. Within a short period, there were Spanish settlers in the

Caribbean and in the northeast of the continent. Stories began to filter back to Spain of vast treasures in the new lands, and many adventurers were tempted to undertake the hazardous journey in search of wealth. One such person was Francisco Pizarro, a Spaniard in his mid-fifties who had failed to achieve anything of note in his homeland.

With a partner, Diego de Almagro, Pizarro organized an expedition in the early 1500s to the New World only to discover that the lands which comprise present-day Mexico had already been stripped of any worthwhile treasure. He undertook many fruitless expeditions in various parts of the Americas but achieved relatively little. However, there were persistent rumors of a civilization located in the Andes Mountains which possessed fabulous wealth. In 1528, Pizarro secured an agreement from the Spanish king that he could be the governor of any new lands he discovered in exchange for which Spain would receive one-fifth of any treasure he found. Pizarro set off for the Andes Mountains with an absurdly small force of fewer than 200 men.

On paper, Pizarro stood no chance at all—to challenge the most powerful empire in South America with such a pitiful force seemed a suicidal venture, but the Incas had already been severely weakened by the arrival of the Spanish. This had not happened through conflict, but due to the diseases which the Spanish had brought with them. Diseases such as smallpox and typhus were unknown in the Americas before the arrival of Europeans, and the local people had no immunity to them. Even diseases such as measles and chickenpox, which were rarely fatal to Europeans, devastated indigenous populations.

The Taino people on the island of Hispaniola, for example, numbered around eight million when Columbus landed there in the late 1400s. Thirty years later, there were just five hundred left. Other indigenous populations suffered similar fates. In April of 1520, Spanish forces landed at Veracruz in present-day Mexico, intending to attack the Aztec Empire. They brought with them modern weapons and at least one person carrying smallpox. By the time that they occupied the Aztec capital Tenochtitlán, around half the population were dead and the streets were littered with the dead and the dying.

The Inca Empire, though it had not been directly invaded at that time, also suffered. The road system proved to be an efficient vector for the new diseases which traders brought with them. By the time that Francisco Pizarro set off for the Andes, disease had already killed an estimated 50-90% of the population of Inca lands (both the Sapa Inca Huayna Capac and his son and heir Ninan Cuyochi are thought to have died of smallpox). Added to the destruction and death caused by the civil war between the forces of Atahualpa and Huáscar, the once mighty Inca Empire was already on its knees before the Spanish arrived.

On Friday, November 15, 1532, Pizarro and his small force arrived in the Inca town of Cajamarca in present-day Peru. Waiting for him was the Sapa Inca accompanied by an army of 80,000 men. He could have seen little threat in the tiny Spanish army. The two men met, and there were discussions, speeches, and drinking. Then, both retired to consider their next moves. Pizarro decided to attack the vast Inca army and set up an ambush in the main square of the town. The following day, the Incas returned and the

Spanish attacked. The Incas suffered around 7,000 soldiers killed. The Spanish, none. Spears and bows proved no match for soldiers equipped with armor and modern firearms. Atahualpa was captured and taken prisoner.

Pizarro demanded a ransom for the Sapa Inca's safe return. He demanded that a large room must be entirely filled with treasure to ensure his release. The Incas agreed, and for eight months, relays of Inca workers brought gold and precious items from all over the empire until the room was finally filled. Then, Pizarro had Atahualpa executed. He used the treasure delivered by the Incas to hire more troops and turned his attention to the city of Cuzco, which he believed held even greater treasure.

The Spanish began to move towards the Inca capital, looting Inca storehouses on the way. They were welcomed by some tribes who saw this as an opportunity to throw off the oppression of the Inca Empire. Cuzco fell to Pizarro's men on November 15, 1533, virtually without a fight. He immediately began stripping the treasures of the city, including the fabulous Coricancha. The incredible artifacts created by a succession of Sapa Incas were stripped from palaces and melted down, and the gold and precious stones shipped out of Cuzco.

Chapter Seven

The Fall of the Inca Empire

"The Incas, although an authoritarian monarchy, had succeeded nevertheless during their short reign not only in creating a massive empire, but perhaps more importantly in guaranteeing all of the empire's millions of inhabitants the basic necessities of life: adequate food, water, and shelter. It was an achievement that no subsequent government—Spanish or Peruvian—has attained since."

—Kim MacQuarrie, The Last Days of the Incas

Although Pizarro and his small force occupied Cuzco, it was apparent that they lacked the resources to exert effective control over the huge empire. Pizarro feared that the disintegration of the empire might make the conquered lands more difficult to control, so he installed a puppet ruler, Túpac Huallpa, a younger brother of Athualpar, as the new Sapa Inca.

The new ruler proved incapable of enforcing order in the rapidly disintegrating empire, and he soon died of smallpox. He was quickly replaced by Manco Inca, a son of Huayna Capac. Initially, the new Sapa Inca seemed content to rule on behalf of the Spanish while Pizarro and his troops attempted to crush remaining resistance, mainly focused in the northern reaches of the empire. They maintained a garrison of 100 men in Cuzco and established a new stronghold in Cuidad de Los Reyes (present-day Lima).

The new Sapa Inca proved less compliant than the Spanish had hoped and Manco Inca led a rebellion against the Spanish occupiers. He escaped from Cuzco and gathered an army of over 200,000 men with which, in 1536, he besieged Cuzco and Cuidad de Los Reyes. However, the Inca armies were not skilled in siege warfare and they were mainly composed of farmers who could not afford to be away from home during the planting or harvest seasons, so the sieges were abandoned. The following year, the Incas returned once again and laid siege to the two Spanish-controlled cities. Once again the Incas were not able to rout the Spanish defenders, and Manco Inca was forced to retreat with his army to the remote jungles of Vilcabamba where he founded a new city which would become the center of what became known as the Neo-Inca State.

From his new city, Manco Inca fought a largely ineffective guerilla war against the Spanish in the mountains and jungles surrounding the Chontabamba River. Meanwhile, Francisco Pizarro had fallen out with his former partner, Diego de Almagro, over the division of Inca treasure. In 1538, Almagro attacked and occupied the city of Cuzco. Pizarro sent his half-brother Hernando to retake the city and Almagro was captured and executed. In 1541, Pizarro was assassinated by killers hired by supporters of Almagro who then fled to Vilcabamba where they sought the protection of Manco Inca. In 1544, these Spaniards murdered Manco Inca and were themselves killed by Inca troops.

One of Manco Inca's sons, Sayri Tupac, then became leader, and in 1558, he finally ended the war with the Spanish and moved to Cuzco where he died in 1561, possibly as a result of being poisoned. He was succeeded by his brother Titu Cusi. The new Sapa Inca remained in Vilcabamba and ruled over what remained of the Incas during an uneasy peace with the Spanish.

When he died in 1571, he was succeeded by Tupac Amaru who would be the last leader of the Incas. In early 1572, two Spanish ambassadors were killed when they attempted to visit Vilcabamba, though it is not known whether this was done on the orders of the new Sapa Inca. In response, the new Spanish Viceroy, Francisco de Toledo, Count of Oropesa, declared war on the Neo-Inca State. On June 24, the Spanish entered the city of Vilcabamba and found that it had been virtually destroyed and that its people, including the Sapa Inca, had fled into the jungle. With the fall of Vilcabamba, the last remnants of the Inca Empire had been destroyed.

The Spanish were determined to ensure that the Incas would never again be able to revolt, and troops were sent to scour the jungles for fugitive Inca nobles and military leaders. Tupac Amaru had left the city with around 100 of his military leaders and members of his extended family. The group then split up to avoid detection, and the Sapa Inca took his heavily pregnant wife along the Masahuay River. A few days later, a group of 40 Spanish soldiers discovered the Sapa Inca and his wife huddled around a small campfire.

The Sapa Inca and his generals, who had also been captured, were brought first to the ruins of Vilcabamba and were then marched back to the city of Cuzco where they arrived in September 1572. The Inca generals were tortured for information on any remaining Inca forces (though there were none). Several died, and the survivors were hanged soon after arriving in Cuzco. On September 24, Tupac Amaru was beheaded in the square in Cuzco, bringing to an end the history of the Inca Empire. In less than 40 years after its first contact with the Spanish invaders, the Inca Empire had gone from being the most powerful in South America to complete and utter destruction.

The only visible legacies left by the Incas today are their monumental buildings, their roads, and their direct descendants—around ten million Quechua-speaking people who live in the high Andes valleys of Peru, Bolivia, and Ecuador. Because they left no written records, we know very little about these people—even the histories that we have were largely written by their Spanish conquerors. Because of this, the Incas have become one of the most fascinating and most mysterious of ancient civilizations.

Conclusion

By the early 1500s, the Inca Empire was vast and powerful, but it was also much more fragile than it appeared from the outside. Partly, this was because it was relatively new and had been established so quickly. This meant that many of the millions of subjects ruled by the Incas still remembered how it was to live independently and many hoped to return to that state. When the Spanish arrived to challenge Inca military supremacy, many of these people seized the opportunity to rebel, and what had looked like a huge, monolithic empire quickly disintegrated back into its constituent elements.

The other reason for the empire's fragility was the fact that it had arisen in isolation, separated from other, different cultures. Inca notions of warfare were ritualized and formal and used weapons and tactics that had changed little from the Stone Age. When fighting other indigenous people, this was sufficient. When faced by the modern weapons and tactics of the Spanish, Inca armies proved to be astonishingly vulnerable.

Its swift destruction and lack of a written Inca language means that this remains one of the most mysterious of civilizations. We still have no idea how the Incas were able to quarry, work, and transport huge blocks of stone nor how they were able to fit these together so perfectly that no mortar was needed to create impregnable walls. We don't know how the Inca were able to perform successful surgery on the skull long before such a thing was possible in Europe. Even the *quipu*, the arrangements of string and knots which the Incas used as recording devices, have never been deciphered.

The Incas were exceptional administrators, successful military campaigners, and great innovators. However, when faced with an external threat for which they were unprepared, they found themselves reduced to the role of subject people in a very short space of time. The rise of the Inca Empire was astonishingly rapid, but its fall was even more abrupt.

Printed in Great Britain
by Amazon